Revise an

Secretarial Duties 2

Geoffrey Whitehead BSc(Econ)

Series Adviser: Geoffrey Whitehead BSc(Econ)

Pitman

PITMAN PUBLISHING LIMITED
128 Long Acre, London WC2E 9AN

A Longman Group Company

© Geoffrey Whitehead 1986

First published in Great Britain 1986

British Library Cataloguing in Publication Data
Whitehead, Geoffrey
  Secretarial duties.—(Revise and test)
  2.
  1. Secretaries—Problems, exercises, etc.
  2. Office practice—Problems, exercises, etc.
  I. Title II. Series
  651.3'741'076   HF5547.5

  ISBN 0-273-02469-8

Printed in Great Britain at The Bath Press, Avon

Contents

Using this Revise and Test booklet

1   The Revise and Test series is in question and answer form. It will teach you everything you need to know (we hope) about your particular syllabus. The questions are detailed and rigorous, and cannot be answered always with one word answers. It follows that the first time you go over a topic you will be learning the material rather than testing yourself. It is not just a self-testing book, but a self-teaching book too!

2   The first time you study a topic you may need to go over it 2 or 3 times. Then put a tick against the topic number in the check list at the back of the book.

3   Subsequently you should revise the topic at intervals, especially just before a monthly test or an examination. Each time you revise it put a further tick.

4   If you find a topic particularly difficult put a ring round the number. This will remind you to do it again soon. Practice makes perfect.

5   Finally remember that learning facts is relatively easy. Applying them in written work is more difficult. Each topic has one piece of written work and you should find others from textbooks and past examination papers. Remember the saying 'Writing maketh an exact man'. Don't worry about who is going to mark your written work. You can appraise it for yourself! Keep writing!

Note: This book is the second of two books entitled Revise and Test Sec- retarial Duties. *If you wish to complete your revision you should also study* Book 1, *which is available from all good booksellers.*

1 Filing – 1: alphabetical filing

1 What is filing?

The storage of documents.

2 What are the principles of filing?

(a) To keep new correspondence in a 'miscellaneous' file until about 6 items of correspondence have accumulated. At this point it is worth opening up a file. (b) Correspondence should be placed in a file folder with a clear title. (c) This folder will then be filed in a suspension folder. (d) The suspension folder will be labelled and inserted at an appropriate point in the classification system being used. (e) Before any folder is removed from its suspension folder it should be replaced by an 'OUT' marker saying who has removed it and why. A date for return should be set. (f) The filing supervisor should chase 'out' files on the due date to secure their return. Meanwhile new correspondence should be kept in a temporary file with the 'out' marker.

3 Who dictates filing policy?

It must be laid down at a high level (a Board review of policy should be held from time to time). The system should not be changed without serious study – a known system is better than erratic changes. The Chief Administration Officer, through a filing supervisor, may be the appropriate person to control policy.

4 What particular policies need to be defined?

(a) Is the system to be centralised or departmental? (b) Is it to be classified alphabetically, numerically, geographically or by subject? (c) Cross-referencing and follow-up procedures. (d) Retention policy, destruction policy and archiving policy.

5 What are the rules for filing alphabetically?

(i) Each name can be divided up into **indexing units**. (ii) The first indexing unit is then selected. This is the surname of a personal name. With impersonal names it is the indexing unit that distinguishes the name from all other names (i.e. Corporation of Lloyds – Lloyds is the one that is chosen – Lloyds, Corporation of). (iii) 'Nothing comes before something', and 'Short before long', i.e. Girton comes before Girton, P. and Girton, P. comes before Girton, Peter. (iv) 'If the first letters are the same the next letters decide', e.g. Gold, Guerdler and Garth are filed Garth, Gold, Guerdler. (v) Titles, decrees and decorations are not indexing units. They are placed after the name, but are ignored, e.g. Grant, Sir George, Grant, Mrs Rebecca. (vi) Names with prefixes are treated as if the prefix was part of the first indexing unit, i.e. Van Gelder is filed under V and Da Vinci under D. (vii) Double-barrelled names are treated as two separate indexing units, unless the hyphenated word is really one word. So Peters-Smythe is filed under Peters, but Ultra-sound Ltd, under Ultra-sound (all one indexing unit). (viii) Separate word names are treated as separate indexing units, i.e. Get You There Travel has four indexing units all of equal importance and would be filed under 'Get'.

Written Exercise: *File each of these sets of three names in correct order: (a) T. Miles, P. Filton, K. Gardham; (b) R. Giles, S. Granger, M. Gerdon; (c) B. Walker, P. Wurlitzer, Sir Peter Whyte-Palmer; (d) Bedford County Council, Council of Physical Recreation, Council for the Blind.*

2 Filing – 2: other filing

1 What is the basis of numerical filing?

(a) It is number based and therefore has more divisions than alphabetical filing.
(b) It is indirect – you can't go to the file at once. You must know the file number and this may mean consulting an index.
(c) You can have a **consecutive digit system**, i.e. drawers labelled 1–50, 51–100, 101–150, etc., or you can have a **terminal digit system**. Letters go in the filing drawer with the same terminal digit as their own. This spreads the new work out over ten drawers. Therefore active files are not all in the same drawer.

2 Explain the numerical file – mark 27:16:04

The last number is the filing cabinet, the fourth filing cabinet, the 16 is the file in the cabinet, and the 27 is the document's place in that file. So the document is the 27th letter in the 16th file in cabinet No 4.

3 What is geographical filing?

Filing based on the country, or within a country it may be based on the county. It is used for sales areas, export departments, etc.
   It is alphabetical within the geographical system.

4 What is subject filing?

Filing done by subjects – as for example a General Administration Office might file under Premises, Staffing, Insurance, Equipment, Maintenance Contracts, etc.
   In such a system we might need primary and secondary guides to help locate the records.

5 What is chronological order filing?

Filing correspondence in date order. It is usual to put today's letter on the top of the correspondence in the file, so that older letters are below. If we know roughly when a letter was received we can search through the file.

6 What are primary and secondary guides?

Guide cards that stick up above the files to show where new areas begin. For example a section on Maintenance Contracts might have a primary guide with a tab reading Maintenance Contracts and then a series of secondary guides reading Heating, Lighting, Telephones, Lifts, etc.

7 What are 'Out' markers?

Marking devices of several types which tell the filing clerk that a file is out, and who has it. Some 'out' cards have a place to write who has the file. Others have a pocket for the request slip – when a file is requested and sent to the person requiring it, the request slip stays with the 'out' marker and is available to help trace the file. Some systems use a 'files out daybook' to record files taken out and upon their return later.

8 Why is cross-referencing important in any filing system?

(a) Many names are multi-word names, and some people may request a file differently from others, i.e. Air Charter Co, or Charter Co (Air). (b) Some firms are subsidiaries of other firms, and their parent company's file may be important as well as their own. (c) Foreign names may be misunderstood and requested differently.

9 How can we cross-reference files?

(a) We may cross-reference the index, i.e. Air Charter Co (see also Charter Co (Air)). (b) We may cross-reference the file covers, i.e. Supercool Ltd (see also Refrigerated Container Services Ltd). (c) We may take photocopies of letters and file them in both files so each is complete.

10 What is a 'follow-up' system?

A system to follow-up 'out' files and secure their return to the filing system. We may have: (a) a 'daily-scan' system, in which we scan the files out each day to detect overdue ones; (b) a tickler system like the 'desk secretary' – see Topic 13 in Book 1. With a tickler system you are reminded each day that something has to be done, because a slip of paper in the system tickles your memory about it.

Written Exercise: *The problem in any filing system is to retrieve a file for use when it is required. How is the problem made worse by: (a) 'out' files; (b) inadequate cross-referencing?*

Go over the topic again until you are sure of all the answers. Then tick it off on the check list at the back of the book.

3 Sources of information – 1: general reference books

1 Why do we need reference books?

Because it is quite impossible to remember all the facts we need to know in everyday life. A well-stacked shelf of reference books clears our minds of clutter – we don't need to wrestle with remembering things when we can look them up in ten seconds.

2 Some people like to display their retentive memories – and constantly show off how clever they are in this respect. What is the best attitude to this type of behaviour?

Polite indifference. The brain is a computer; its central processing unit is best kept clear of unnecessary details. Just as a computer keeps its memory in peripheral units we keep the vast majority of our memories on the reference bookshelf.

3 What are the chief general reference books?

Dictionaries, thesauruses, encyclopaedias, atlases, gazetteers and almanacs.

4 What is the chief use of a dictionary?

It helps us develop our vocabulary, by giving us the meaning of words we did not formerly know, and enabling us to use them in future. It also helps with spelling.

5 What is a thesaurus?

The word means 'treasury' and it is a treasury of words. With a dictionary, we know a word and look up its meaning – with a thesaurus we know the meaning we are after and look up the word.

6 Which is the most famous thesaurus?

Roget's Thesaurus of English Words and Phrases. This is the original one, first published in 1852, and revised and updated ever since.

7 How does a thesaurus work?

You look up the idea you are after in the index of ideas – which is about half the book. Suppose the idea you are thinking of is 'exactness'. You look up 'exact' and find there are fourteen different uses of the word. One of these will be near the idea you have in mind – for example 'precise'. Against the word 'precise' is a reference to the other half of the book, where you will find there are 38 words or phrases which mean 'precise'.

8 What is an encyclopaedia?

A book, or set of books, which covers a huge range of subjects, and gives short accounts of the history, technology, art, literature, science, administration, etc. of the modern world.

9 Name three encyclopaedias suitable for use in the office

The *Encyclopaedia Britannica* is the most famous, but it is very large and fairly expensive. *Chamber's Encyclopaedia* is widely used, and the single volume of *Pears Cyclopaedia* is inexpensive and excellent for general use. It is updated every year – and an annual reorder is a sound idea.

10 Why might we need an encyclopaedia in an office?

Very often we need to prepare briefs (background information) for senior personnel travelling abroad, so that they are familiar with the general history, economic state, political situation, etc. in countries they are visiting.

11 What are the respective uses of (a) atlases and (b) gazetteers?

Atlases help us locate places anywhere in the world and gazetteers give us detailed information about countries, cities, towns and districts in all parts of the world.

Their chief uses are: (a) as a source of correct spelling of foreign place names; (b) in mailing operations; (c) in planning journeys and routes – they may give distances to be travelled; (d) in assessing marketing problems, the location of depots and service areas, etc.; (e) in providing background information for travellers.

12 What is an almanac?

An annual publication, originally giving astronomical data but today extended into an annual reference book on many subjects. The most famous name today is *Whitaker's Almanack* – a comprehensive reference book giving detailed information, particularly about the United Kingdom, the monarchy, peerage, administration, etc.

Written Exercise: *A director of the company you work for is about to travel to Mexico – in particular to the area called Yucatan. Prepare him a short account of Yucatan, and its general position, population, economic resources, etc.*

Go over the topic again until you are sure of all the answers. Then tick it off on the check list at the back of the book.

4 Sources of information – 2: specialist reference books

1 What is a specialist reference book?

A book which deals with the detailed requirements of a particular area of work, or with a particular profession. Such books need updating regularly and therefore may take the form of a year book, or a quarterly, or they may be updated by monthly revision pages on a loose-leaf system.

2 Give examples of year books

The Stock Exchange Year Book, The Haulage Manual (published by the Road Haulage Association), *Lloyd's Calendar* – the annual publication of Lloyd's of London. There are many more.

3 Give examples of specialist manuals with updating services

Some famous ones are the handbooks published by Croner Publications Ltd. Important manuals include *Croner's Reference Book for the Self-Employed, Croner's Reference Book for Employers, Croner's Reference Book for Exporters,* etc. Nearly all the major aspects of business activity are covered by Croner handbooks.

4 What is a directory?

A book which gives names, addresses and other information relevant to a particular area of interest. For example, a telephone directory, classified directories such as *Yellow Pages* and professional directories published by institutes such as the Institute of Chartered Accountants, the Institute of Personnel Management, etc.

5 Name some professional directories

Crockford's Clerical Directory, The Medical Directory, The Law List, The Army List.

6 You have taken employment in a large organisation, and wish to improve your background knowledge of the industry. Where would you seek information?

The logical place is the professional organisation or trade association for that particular industry. Someone on the staff will know who the appropriate body is, who enrols students for courses of professional studies, etc. A brief request for background information, entry qualifications, etc. addressed to the institute or trade association will bring you all the information you need.

7 What is the correct attitude for a young person entering an industry?

To seek at once to take the necessary steps to achieve eventual professional status in the industry. You can usually become a student member of the professional body at once, provided you have basic qualifications. After that, advancement depends upon passing two sets of examinations over a period of between 3 and 5 years. Study is a part-time activity undertaken while you are gaining practical experience. You need both theory and practice.

8 Where do specialist reference books enter into such a programme of work?

They are full of procedures, glossaries of terms used in the industry, safety requirements, legal implications, etc.

9 What is *Who's Who*?

A directory of prominent people in all walks of life; it gives short biographies, qualifications, decorations, etc. and is useful when writing to such individuals and wishing to use the correct title, style of address, etc.

10 What book will assist you with styles of address?

Black's Titles and Forms of Address, gives the correct title, salutation and subscription when writing to persons of rank.

Written Exercise: *Consult your local* Yellow Pages *telephone directory to discover the person nearest to your home who could: (a) fill a cavity in your tooth; (b) replace a leaking radiator in your home; (c) ship your* *furniture to Hong Kong; (d) supply you with a Chinese meal; (e) sell you a motor scooter; (f) advise you about life assurance.*

Go over the topic again until you are sure of all the answers. Then tick it off on the check list at the back of the book.

5 Sources of information – 3: information technology

1 What is information technology?

It is any sort of technology which enables you to receive information from a computerised source, giving instantaneous access to stored data.

2 Where is its most immediate use?

In situations such as travel agencies, dealing with hotel accommodation, etc., where numerous branches can be supplied with information on VDUs and by keying in the necessary details can update the computer to book rooms, seats on aircraft, etc.

3 What is the effect of such a booking?

(a) It secures the accommodation for the customer. (b) It reduces the record of available space by the amount booked, so that other branches seeking accommodation have a reduced choice – and eventually the bookings are full and none is available. (c) It may generate documentation at a later date to complete the ordinary commercial transaction.

4 What is the ACP 80 computer?

It is the computer for London Airport. Heathrow and Gatwick and also several British ports can enter imports and exports at Customs and obtain instantaneous updates on the release of goods for loading or distribution to the hinterland.

5 What are the Ceefax and Oracle systems?

Information services from the BBC and Independent Television networks which can be received by viewers with teletext receivers to give instantaneous screenings of desired information.

6 What is a network?

It is a system which permits authorised users to gain entry to other organisations' computers. By use of a 12-number code which acts as a user identifier, the caller can gain direct access to the computer chosen, use its programs, copy its information and generally take advantage of the services offered. The systems work all over Europe, and North America, and will soon be world-wide.

7 What are Expert Systems or Knowledge Systems?

Computerised systems that have been programmed with all the knowledge on a particular field, such as medicine or business. The caller calls up the computer, tells it the problem and it will print out the most likely solution. Thus a doctor could give the patient's symptoms and the computer would diagnose the illness. These are sometimes called 'artificial intelligence' systems.

8 What is telemetry?

Automatic telephonic transfer of data to specific receiving points for action – as where rivers are tested for oxygen content to reduce fish kills; tides are measured to give advance warning of flood levels; etc.

Written Exercise: *Mrs Smith wishes to take a holiday in Seychelles. What details would the travel agent need to know to make the booking? How could information technology help?*

Go over the topic again until you are sure of all the answers. Then tick it off on the check list at the back of the book.

6 Mail inwards

1 What is the secretary's attitude to incoming mail?

It is essential to co-operate in opening and sorting it, so that the mail for his/her chief can be obtained early in the day for processing.

2 What advantage does co-operation with other secretaries and middle managers (who usually open and sort the mail) bring?

It helps you to know what is happening in other departments, and the staff in those departments.

3 What is the routine for opening incoming mail?

(a) Face the mail – i.e. turn it all round the same way. (b) Take out misdirected mail and return it to the Post Office. (c) Remove personal and confidential mail and put it in the trays of those to whom it is addressed, after date-stamping. (d) Open the rest and sort it into the trays of those best placed to answer it, after date-stamping and checking the contents. (e) Record any incoming remittances in a remittances inwards book. (f) If necessary affix a circulation slip to mail of interest to several people.

4 What is the routine for your chief's mail?

(a) Do not open personal or confidential mail unless this has been agreed beforehand. (b) Sort other mail into: (i) routine matters to be dealt with at once on the basis of agreed arrangements; (ii) more important letters. (c) Read all other letters and arrange them in the order of importance. (d) Get out any relevant files likely to be required in answering the mail. Find the relevant correspondence in the file and label it with a scrap of paper sticking out, i.e. Contract here! Original complaint here!, collection of letters and files – with the confidential letters on top if unopened – on the chief's desk. (f) Deal with the routine matters while waiting for the chief to arrive.

5 One of the letters today is a change of address from an important customer. What must you do?

(a) Update all records in your own office. (b) Attach a circulation slip to the notice and send it on its way to *all* those likely to need to know about it. It is essential not to overlook anyone as this can be very irritating to a good customer.

Written Exercise: *Explain why you should date-stamp all incoming mail. (There are several reasons.)*

Go over the topic again until you are sure of all the answers. Then tick it off on the check list at the back of the book.

7 Mail outwards

1 What is the essential feature about mail outwards?

So far as possible it should be posted early in the day – mail posted early is more likely to reach its destination next day than mail posted in rush hours.

2 What should the secretary do to promote early despatch of mail?

(a) Deal with routine mail early in the day pending the chief's consideration of more important correspondence.
(b) Leave time early in the day on his/her diary for dealing with correspondence – so that appointments do not begin until an early dictation session is over. The secretary can then proceed with the replies. (c) Leave gaps in the diary later in the day – especially if the chief is leaving the building for the day – so that important letters can be signed. (d) Get permission to sign p.p. the executive if he/she is frequently absent.

3 What does p.p. mean?

Per procurationem – it is the Latin for 'by proxy' or 'done by an agent'. The secretary is the agent of the executive. Some secretaries type 'Dictated by XYZ but signed in his absence by permission'.

4 Supposing a secretary works for several executives – what rules are important?

The executives must know the basic deadlines for mail and not habitually deal with mail late in the day. The occasional late emergency letter is one thing; habitual disregard of the secretary's work schedule, personal arrangements and hours of duty is another.

5 How can this sort of arrangement be clarified?

By providing 2 trays, one for non-urgent mail and the other for urgent mail. As the end of the day approaches non-urgent mail will be left until next day. Only urgent mail will be cleared.

6 How may pressure on the Post Department be relieved?

(a) By sending mail down at regular intervals during the day. Every two hours is a suitable time period. This takes the pressure off the end of the day. (b) A secretary who knows late mail is unavoidable may arrange for a letter scale and a small supply of stamps to enable him/her to deal personally with any late letters.

7 What should he/she also do to make this system sound?

Keep a record of such late mail, the executive concerned and the postage paid.

8 What about the quality of mail outwards?

(a) Those in a supervisory role should ensure that it is in good style, correctly spelled and presented. (b) Poor performance by junior staff should be pointed out – and perhaps a retraining programme arranged. Merit increases in pay should not be given to those whose performance is slovenly.

Written Exercise: *What precautions should be taken to avoid excessive build-ups of mail in the Post Department? How could a secretary ensure good relations with the Mail Outwards supervisor?*

Go over the topic again until you are sure of all the answers. Then tick it off on the check list at the back of the book.

8 The pictorial representation of data – 1: charts and diagrams

1 What are the chief types of pictorial representation of data?

(a) Graphs. (b) Pictograms. (c) Bar-charts. (d) Pie charts. (e) Gantt charts. (f) Histograms.

2 Why are graphs so important?

Data is frequently displayed as graphs and these allow rapid assimilation of information. They gave rise to the whole art of graphics. (Topic 9 is devoted to them.)

3 What are pictograms?

These convey statistical facts in picture form. An appropriate symbol is used to represent the data, and the size or number of symbols denotes the quantity involved as shown in Fig. 8.1.

Greece 🍾🍾🍾🍾 ▮ (5.5mhl)

United Kingdom 🍾🍾🍾. (4.25mhl)

Ireland ▪ (0.25mhl)

Italy 🍾🍾🍾🍾🍾 🍾🍾🍾🍾🍾 🍾🍾🍾🍾🍾 🍾🍾🍾🍾🍾(72.25mhl)

Fig. 8.1 Wine consumption in four countries (Source: *Annual Reports: EEC*)

4 What does each symbol (a bottle) display in Fig. 8.1?

One million hectolitres.

5 Explain the principle of the bar chart

Information is related to the horizontal or vertical length of a bar or thick line. The bars are used to compare sets of data. This is shown in Fig. 8.2 in an analysis of turnover in a supermarket.

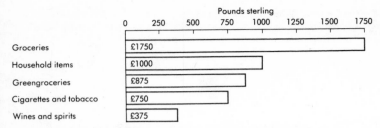

Fig. 8.2 An analysis of turnover in a supermarket (Source: Week 17 Departmental Returns)

6 What are the design features of a bar chart?

(a) The *scale* must be chosen so that all the data can appear easily, i.e. with the largest piece of data using up almost all the scale. (b) The bars should be the same width, since only length is used to denote the data. (c) Bar charts can be drawn horizontally or vertically. (d) Colours or cross-hatching can be helpful in differentiating between the bars. (e) Positive and negative bar charts can be used to show relative changes about a mean or zero, as shown in Fig. 8.3.

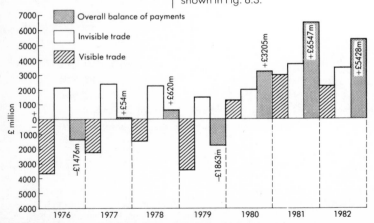

Fig. 8.3 The United Kingdom balance of payments 1976–82 (Source: *The United Kingdom Balance of Payments* (Pink Book))

7 When are multiple bar charts used?

When we wish to compare a number of items over a number of years. They show how each item varies over the period. (An example is given in Fig. 8.4.)

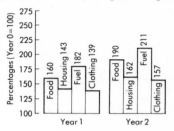

Fig. 8.4 Multiple bar charts for comparing data

8 How would you show totals using a bar chart?

By drawing a component bar chart as shown in Fig. 8.5.

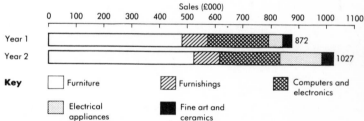

Fig. 8.5 Component bar charts

9 Explain Fig. 8.5

The total sales in each year is shown by the total length of the bar (£872 000 in Year 1 and £1027 000 in Year 2). The individual parts that make up the total are shown by shading, cross-hatching, etc., and can be compared.

10 Describe a percentage bar chart

This is obtained by showing the entire set of statistics as 100 per cent and components calculated as a percentage of the whole (see Fig. 8.6).

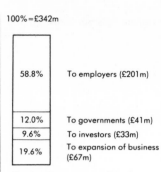

100% = £342m

58.8% — To employers (£201m)

12.0% — To governments (£41m)

9.6% — To investors (£33m)

19.6% — To expansion of business (£67m)

Fig. 8.6 A percentage bar chart on the use of profits

11 Do three-dimensional bar chart representations convey any additional information?

Very rarely, and they make it more difficult to see the end of the bar. They may add to the visual impression, but are awkward to draw quickly in examinations, and should be avoided. An example is given in Fig. 8.7.

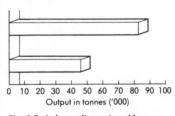

0 10 20 30 40 50 60 70 80 90 100
Output in tonnes ('000)

Fig. 8.7 A three-dimensional bar chart

12 What is a pie chart?

As shown in Fig. 8.8, the round 'pie' is cut up into slices, each of which represents a percentage of the total. The percentage is translated into degrees so that the total is 360°. These degrees have been given in Fig. 8.8 to show how the circle is divided up, but they would usually not appear in the finished pie chart. Instead the percentages of the total would be shown.

UK visible exports

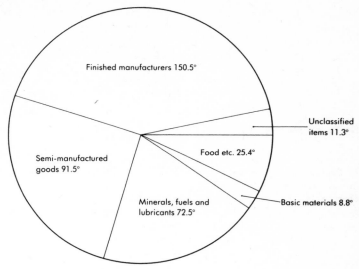

Fig. 8.8 United Kingdom visible exports (Source: *The United Kingdom Balance of Payments* **(Pink Book))**

13 What chart would you use to compare actual and planned performance?

The Gantt chart.

14 How do we display them on a Gantt chart?

The chart consists of a layout of equally spaced columns, each of which represents a week (or month). Planned performance is represented by the full width of the column, and actual performance is filled in across the column as it is achieved. If the other side of the column is not reached we have under-performed, and if performance is greater than planned we start a second line. This is drawn in Fig. 8.9.

	1	2	3	4	5	6
Planned sales (£)	4000	4500	3250	4000	5000	8000
Actual Sales (£)	3400	4250	3800	4750	6250	
% achievement	85%	94.4%	116.9%	118.75%	125%	
Actual achievement						
Cumulative achievement						

Fig. 8.9 A Gantt chart

15 Explain the cumulative achievement line on the Gantt chart

The cumulative achievement line is built up by adding each period's performance to the previous performances. We do have to be a little careful though. The whole point of a Gantt chart is that it is flexible – the planned performances for each period do not have to be the same. For example, sales figures could reflect seasonal changes. We might plan for massive sales in December and very little in January, after the Christmas rush. In building up the cumulative line we have to show the last section of actual achievement as a percentage of the planned performance of that period. In Fig. 8.9 the extra performance achieved in the five months is £1700 sales, which is less than $\frac{1}{4}$ of £8000 – the planned sales in the next period.

16 What is a histogram?

A way of displaying frequency distributions so that they can be easily understood.

17 How is a histogram drawn?

As a series of rectangles each of which represents one class interval. The blocks stand next to one another and show the pattern of the distribution. If the blocks are of uniform width the height of each block is determined by the frequency, as

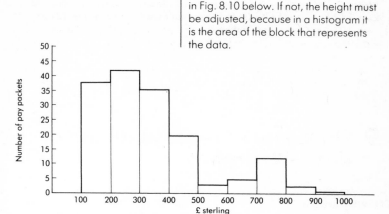

in Fig. 8.10 below. If not, the height must be adjusted, because in a histogram it is the area of the block that represents the data.

Fig. 8.10 A histogram on monthly take home pay

18 What is a frequency polygon?

It is a line drawn on the histogram by joining the midpoints of the tops of the blocks as shown in Fig. 8.11. Each line creates two similar triangles, one of which is included in the polygon and the other excluded. The result is that the area under the polygon is the same as the total area of the blocks.

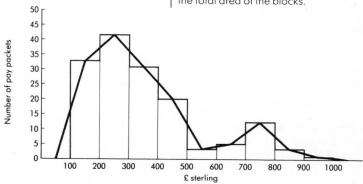

Fig. 8.11 A frequency polygon

Written Exercise: *A United Kingdom firm sells 46 per cent of its goods to Europe, 13 per cent to the USA, 18 per cent to African countries, 12 per cent to India, 7 per cent to Pakistan and the balance to Australia. Draw a pie chart to show its distribution to overseas territories.*

Go over the topic again until you are sure of all the answers. Then tick it off on the check list at the back of the book.

9 The pictorial representation of data – 2: graphs

1 What are graphs?

Graphs are pictorial representations of data which show the relationship between two variables. The variables are plotted against axes called the *x* and *y* ordinates. A scale is chosen to match the data and crosses or some other symbol are used to mark the points on the graph. The points may be joined by a continuous or dotted line or a combination of both if more than one set of data is to be drawn.

2 Explain Fig. 9.1

Figure 9.1 shows sales of newspapers (shown as the *y* ordinate) plotted against quarters of the year (shown as the *x* ordinate). The sales of each paper are joined by different types of lines to differentiate them for the reader. They indicate that the *Daily Pictorial* has overtaken the *Daily News* in the three-year period shown.

3 What does the zig-zag line at the foot of the *y* axis indicate in Fig. 9.1?

That the scale has been interrupted. Since both papers sold more than 3 million copies there was no point in showing the sales below that figure. The vertical scale is interrupted between 0 and 3 to highlight data variations.

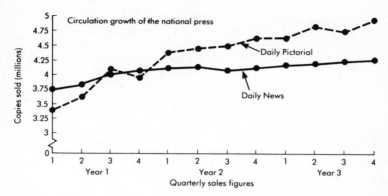

Fig. 9.1 A graph with an interrupted scale

4 What is Fig. 9.2? It is a *Z* chart.

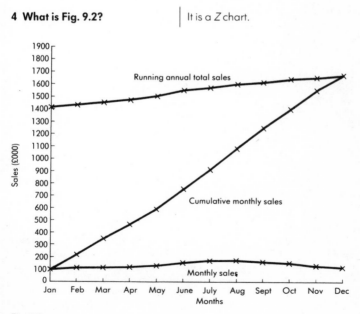

Fig. 9.2

5 Explain what a Z chart is

It is frequently used by selling organisations to plot current, cumulative and annual figures. The result finishes up as a rather erratically shaped Z curve, as shown in Fig. 9.2. The bottom line shows current monthly sales. The top line shows a moving cumulative total of sales for the previous 12 months. The oblique line shows the cumulative total for the current year to date. The Z must join up in the last month of the year because the total for the year to date then becomes the same as the total for the last 12 months.

6 What type of graph is Fig. 9.3?

A layered graph.

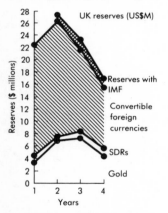

Fig. 9.3 (Source: *The United Kingdom Balance of Payments* (Pink Book))

7 How is a layered graph obtained?

Quite often data consists of component parts of a grand total. Total sales of a firm would be made up of sales from several departments or the official reserves of the United Kingdom are made up of several types of finances, as shown in Fig. 9.3. As gold is heavy, we show it as the bottom layer. The second layer – IMF special drawing rights – is then added and further layers are superimposed until the total United Kingdom reserves have been obtained as the top line on the graph.

8 What sort of graph is Fig. 9.4?

A straight-line graph through the origin.

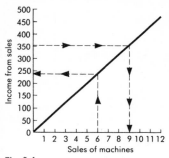

Fig. 9.4

9 What does this type of graph show?

It shows a constant relationship between two variables. From such a graph we can interpolate (find the value of any point on the graph). For example we can read off the income from any volume of sales by simply drawing a vertical line from the horizontal axis to intercept the graph then drawing a horizontal line from the intercept point to the y axis.

10 What is extrapolation?

Reading off the value of a point not on the graph as drawn, but on an extension of the graph, to predict the future sales, etc.

11 Why is extrapolation sometimes misleading?

Because when we extrapolate outside the range of the graph we cannot be sure that the straight-line relationship still holds. It does not follow that because 10 machines can be sold for £400 we can earn £400 000 by selling 10 000 of them. We may have to lower the selling price to achieve the larger volume of sales.

12 What is the general expression for a straight line graph showing a relationship between two variables *x* and *y*?

$y = a + bx$

13 Will such a graph pass through the origin?

Only if *a*, the constant term, is 0.

14 What does *a* decide in the formula $y = a + bx$?

The intercept on the *y* axis, so if *a* is zero, the intercept will be at the origin of the graph.

15 What does *b* decide in the formula $y = a + bx$?

The slope of the graph. It is the extent to which *y* changes with respect to *x*.

16 What sort of graph is Fig. 9.5 below?

A breakeven chart.

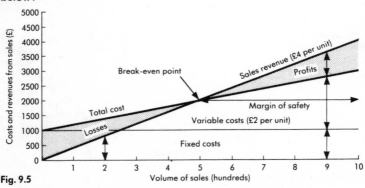

Fig. 9.5

17 What purpose do breakeven charts serve?

They provide a means of assessing the effect of pricing policy and fixed variable costs on profitability. Figure 9.5 shows the total costs made up of a fixed costs (e.g., building costs) plus variable costs (e.g., operating costs) and the total revenue obtained from sales. The point where the two lines cross is called the breakeven point where costs and revenue are equal. Operating to the right of this point gives us an overall profit – to the left produces a net loss.

18 How can we emphasise the relative importance of two variables?

By rewriting the data in cumulative percentage terms and then plotting the new data set for the variables against each other, we obtain a Lorenz curve.

19 Explain the Lorenz curve in Fig. 9.6 which is about the distribution of incomes in the country of Espaniona

(a) The straight line is the locus of points where income is being equally distributed. (b) Since our data points are far from this line they indicate that income is not evenly distributed (only 37 per cent of income is earned by 94 per cent of the population). (c) Espaniona is clearly a country where the rich are very rich and many people are rather poor. (50 per cent of the population have about 14 per cent of the income.)

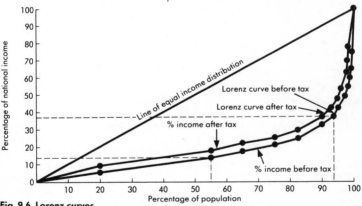

Fig. 9.6 Lorenz curves

Written Exercise: *A firm has fixed costs of £20 000 and variable costs of £10 per unit of output. Each unit is sold for £20. Draw a graph of output and sales in steps of 1000 up to 5000 units. Where is the breakeven point?*

Go over the topic again until you are sure of all the answers. Then tick it off on the check list at the back of the book.

10 Executive travel – 1: first considerations

1 Why do executives need to travel?

Because in the modern world everyone uses raw materials, components and finished products from all over the world. We need to travel to obtain the supplies we need and to market our products. We also need to experience the actual conditions our goods are sold in.

2 Give an example of the latter

The goods we supply to foreigners have to be in marketable condition. Ordinary fat may melt in the tropics and we need to develop high melting point fats. Arctic conditions call for low melting point fats that 'spread straight from the fridge'.

We need to see the actual transport being used – no good sending a 32-ton container if all they have at the other end are wheelbarrows.

3 What is important in planning executive travel?

(a) Know why the visit is being made.
(b) Know what it is hoped to achieve.
(c) Know who is likely to be visited.
(d) Establish linking arrangements so both the executive and the secretary can always get in touch. (e) Think the whole process through and arrange the practical details at every stage. (f) Make arrangements to cover for the executive while he/she is away.

4 Where does the planning begin?

With preliminary discussions about the purpose of the visit, the places to be visited, the people to be interviewed and the aims to be achieved in each section of the journey.

5 What follows from this?

More detailed planning of each section including: (a) Who do we hope to meet; (b) Will he/she be available – book appointments and confirm arrangements; (c) What data and information will be discussed – prepare a pack of information, data, brochures or other material to brief the executives on each place, interview, etc.; (d) Envisage follow-up activities – so the executive can off-load each part of the work as it is completed and move on to the next stage with a clear head; (e) Plan the actual details of accommodation, etc.; (f) Start to build up a cost-budget to provide for all the funds needed.

6 What is an itinerary?

It is a plan for a journey showing the dates and times of each stage of the journey – the meetings to be held, the travel necessary, the factories or depots or offices to be visited, etc.

7 Why is it important not to have too tight a schedule?

(a) Because foreign travel is always rather unreliable – weather may be unfavourable, etc. (b) Because customers or suppliers hope to make friends and show off their country, its sights and special features. These events cannot be rushed. (c) Because the pace of life may be slower, and it is best to 'flow with the rest' rather than battle your way through a series of obstructions and difficulties.

8 What are the particular problems of foreign travel?

(a) Public holidays are different and should be checked out by reference to the 'country' pages of handbooks like *Croner's Handbook for Exporters*. (b) Visas may be required and must be arranged well beforehand. (c) Foreign currency has to be obtained and acceptable travellers cheques, credit cards, etc., should be obtained.

9 What about the actual travel arrangements?	Once your itinerary is clear see a travel agent and get him/her to do all the travel preparations. This is not expensive, and agents have all the links and computerised connections to any place in the world. It will be a nightmare for you but enjoyable for them.
10 Why 'enjoyable' for them?	Because much of their work is rather repetitive and boring – the same old holidays to the same old places. Executive travel arrangements are more of a challenge, and they will enjoy booking tickets for obscure up-country places that are a little unusual.
11 All work and no play makes Jack a dull boy and Jill a dull girl. How will the travel agents help here?	They will know what sights are worth seeing, what entertainments are available. They will book tickets, arrange functions, help you to reciprocate the entertainment you receive by booking restaurant facilities, etc.
12 What supplies might an executive need?	(a) Visiting cards. (b) Sales or other promotional literature. (c) Customers' records or records of output at factories, plantations, etc. Possibly accountants' reports, lawyers' opinions, technical reports, etc. (d) Visit briefs. (e) Prepared speeches for various occasions. (f) Lists of names, addresses, telephone numbers, etc. (g) Prepared post-cards or letters to be posted ahead to the next stage of the journey reminding people of his/her arrival, etc.
13 How should these materials be supplied?	Preferably in packs in itinerary order – so that each set is not muddled with other material but is only opened when the executive reaches that stage of the journey.

Written Exercise: *You are making preparations for your executive to travel*

to Singapore and Malaya where your firm has widespread interests. Refer to a map of the area and list five main centres which can be used as meeting places. Then use a gazetteer to find out background information on the towns concerned.

Go over the topic again until you are sure of all the answers. Then tick it off on the check list at the back of the book.

11 Executive travel – 2: detailed arrangements

1 What is a visit brief?

It is a package of information which will be of use to an executive in a particular section of a journey – say a visit to a particular factory, depot or branch.

2 What does it consist of?

A briefing on each aspect that is likely to be of interest. For example a breakdown of past performance, the trend in production or sales – strong points on which praise is possible and weaknesses which should be probed. Briefs about particular problems, or troublesome individuals, or potential difficulties likely to arise if management proposals meet criticism, etc., etc.

3 How does the executive use the visit brief?

He/she reads it all through before setting off and discusses it with anyone on the staff who knows the place, its problems and potential. Then it is read again the night before the actual visit – and any more recent developments notified are incorporated into the package. There might be a prepared report included which enables the executive to complete a full account of the current position by completing boxes or spaces on the report after the interview. This could be posted back to Head Office or, even better, sent by facsimile copier. It only takes 20 seconds per page to send back over the telephone system a complete copy of the executive's conclusions.

4 Why is it desirable to have prepared speeches ready for delivery?

(a) Because many executives do not know all about the places to be visited and someone on the staff may be able to help a great deal in making a speech more relevant to the country concerned. (b) Because foreigners may be sensitive about certain aspects of their way of life and it is essential to avoid saying the wrong thing. (c) Because even if the executive later modifies the wording to suit the developments taking place during his visit the prepared speech will give a useful basis for the final speech. (d) Most major speeches by top personnel are released beforehand to the press – on the understanding that they don't print anything until after the speech is delivered. This gives them the chance to set the type ready – and get it correct without relying on a reporter's scribbled notes.

5 What are the back-up elements required for any overseas visit?

(a) The secretary (if not travelling with the executive) must be able to make contact with him/her every day. It is wise to fix a time of at least an hour each day when the executive will be available in the hotel. (b) An 'immediate-action' routine should be devised to deal with urgent problems like the fulfilment of orders, the modification of arrangements, etc. (c) Someone should be appointed to stand in for the executive and handle his/her current work, as well as to appraise any correspondence or dictated material airmailed back to Head Office, or facsimile copied or telexed to Head Office. (If you haven't a facsimile copier or a telex see your local Telecom representative who will arrange to receive messages at a local bureau, where you can collect them.) (d) The secretary should be willing to take calls day and night if the time-lag is very great. Singapore is 7 hours different, for example; noon in Singapore is 5 a.m. in London.

6 What personal matters need attending to well in advance?

(a) Passports, visas, international driving licence, health certificates, inoculations and any special health requirements such as insulin for diabetics, tablets for heart patients, etc. (b) Any necessary letters of identification and introduction should be prepared. (c) Appropriate clothing, footwear, recreational wear, etc. (d) Spare spectacles are essential for those with poor sight. A whole visit can be ruined if the traveller cannot see, or looks ridiculous because spectacles are held together with adhesive tape. (e) There are many things the executive should do before he/she leaves – or things to be done while he/she is away. Family events, business courtesies to be performed, etc.

7 What needs to happen on Departure Day Minus One?

The secretary should go over the whole visit with the executive, explaining each visit pack, the full itinerary, the availability of materials already sent ahead by air freight, the list of addresses, telephone numbers, etc.

Go through the contents of the executive's briefcase and explain where everything is – especially travel documents, itinerary (with spare copies), check lists for each visit (as included in the visit brief pack). A final check list should be given to the executive for use before he/she leaves for the airport next day.

Written Exercise: *You are about to go on a journey for your firm leaving your secretary to keep general control of your work while you are away. Suggest the arrangements you should make about: (a) Very important matters which the secretary could not be expected to deal with; (b) Routine matters of an everyday nature; (c) A daily contact between the secretary and yourself; (d) What to do in the event of your death abroad.*

Go over the topic again until you are sure of all the answers. Then tick it off on the check list at the back of the book.

12 Executive travel – 3: more about travel arrangements

1 What are the chief methods of travel for executives these days?

Air travel is predominant. Sea travel would only be used if an executive wanted to combine a holiday (a cruise) with business meetings at the end of the journey. Rail travel is still important for long inland journeys, but the car is the chief means of inland transport.

2 What publication gives full details of air travel?

The ABC World Airways Guide – but it is much better (and probably cheaper) to leave all travel arrangements to a specialist travel agent, who has the backing of modern technology.

3 In what way does this help?

With on-line computer links to all carriers and hotels, and even to Customs if goods or samples have to be sent ahead, the travel agent is well placed to handle all aspects within seconds.

4 What reference book provides details of rail travel?

The ABC Railway Guide gives times of train departures and arrivals throughout Britain. British Rail timetables give routes of trains and the stations at which they call, and details of shipping services connected with British Rail.

5 What books are helpful in planning journeys by car?

The AA and RAC handbooks. Also *Hotels and Restaurants in Britain*, published by the British Travel Association.

6 What arrangements should be made about money for overseas travel?

(a) A small supply of local currency should be ordered from the bank. Travellers returning home should give in their small change (which is useful for tips, etc.), for use by the next visitor who goes out. (b) Traveller's cheques should be arranged for the various countries to be visited (your bank will advise about problem areas). (c) Credit card facilities (with adequate reserves on the card) should be taken. (d) Links with London branches of foreign banks might be worth while establishing – the embassy of the country concerned will advise the names of national banks. The foreign branches of British banks will offer the same services.

7 What arrangements are necessary re passports, etc.?

(a) The executive should have a full passport – not just a visitor's passport. (b) Forms are available at any Post Office, and as passports take some time to arrange, except in a genuine emergency, apply in good time. (c) Visas may be necessary for each country concerned. These also take time to arrange, so apply early to the embassy concerned.

8 What handbook is helpful for details about any country in the world?

Croner's Reference Book for Exporters has 'country' pages for every country in the world giving a great many details helpful to business travellers abroad.

9 What insurance is advisable?

(a) Cover against loss of personal belongings. (b) Cover against personal accident, medical and hospital expenses, etc. (c) A life assurance policy in favour of dependants is desirable. We are all worth more than we imagine, so a good cover is required – say at least £100 000.

10 What health precautions should be taken?

Your doctor will advise, or the embassy will tell you of any specific requirements for inoculations, etc.

Written Exercise: *Choose any country in the world. Go to the library and consult* **Croner's Reference Book for Exporters** *and hence discover the variety of relevant facts on the 'country' page. Write a short report on the special points an executive should know.*

Go over the topic again until you are sure of all the answers. Then tick it off on the check list at the back of the book.

13 Reprography

1 What is reprography?

It is the process of reproducing documents so that everyone who needs a copy can have one.

2 What methods are available?

Today the plain paper copier is almost universal, but there are many other methods, such as photocopying, stencil copying, facsimile copying, carbon copying, offset printing and spirit duplicating.

3 How has reprography developed in recent years?

In particular by the setting up in almost all large organisations of in-house printing departments to produce documents, display materials, house journals, etc.

4 What is a master copy?

It is the document from which copies are made. It may be a letter, art-work of some sort, or a specialised master such as a stencil for stencil duplicating.

5 Why is an accurate master essential?

Because any error in a master will be reproduced in every copy, and instead of correcting one master we shall have to correct every copy made.

6 What is the rule about making a master copy then?

(a) Take great care to produce it.
(b) Think through every detail – does it need a date, a time, a venue (meeting place), etc? Has every necessary detail been included? Is every spelling correct, etc? (c) Get someone else to check it – two heads are better than one.

7 Supposing a good master produces poor copies. What is the problem?

Every duplicating or copying machine needs servicing regularly. Call in the representative and have the machine serviced.

8 What factors influence the choice of a reprographic system?

(a) The number of copies required.
(b) The speed with which you need them.
(c) The nature of the service – has everyone access to the machine, or is there to be a specialist operator? (d) Do we require coloured copies? (e) The running costs of the machine. (f) The quality of the product required – cheap and cheerful or highly professional.

9 What is the difference between a copier and a duplicator?

A duplicator requires a specially prepared master, such as a spirit master, a stencil, a paper plate or a metal plate.

10 Explain how the plain paper copier works

(a) The original copy is laid on a glass sheet called a platen. (b) A traversing device causes the copy to move relative to the copying paper. (c) An electrostatic charge appears to reproduce the material to be copied.

(d) This charge takes up a powder or liquid toner. (e) The copy is then fixed to the paper by either a heating process or a chemical process.

11 What is xerography?

It is the original plain paper copying. Xero means 'dry' and this name was used to distinguish electrostatic copying from photocopying, which needed wet developers.

12 Why is photocopying little used today?

(a) Because the special photographic paper has a short life. (b) The copies are more expensive and less pleasant to handle and the machines are slower.

13 What are the advantages of copying machines over duplicating machines?

(a) They are convenient (copies can be made at any time). (b) They are foolproof (anyone can press a button). (c) They are quick (up to 2 copies a second) and (d) adaptable (copies can be made from anything – books, magazines, correspondence, documents, photographs).

14 What is collation?

The process of arranging pages in order to make sets for stapling reports, in-house magazines, etc.

15 What is a collating machine?

An additional machine provided in conjunction with a copier which collates papers into sets automatically, for stapling.

Written Exercise: *Visit a resource centre, copy shop or print shop and study the procedure for plain paper copying. Write a short evaluation of the procedure, its likely cost per copy produced, etc.*

Go over the topic again until you are sure of all the answers. Then tick it off on the check list at the back of the book.

14 More about reprography

1 What is offset duplicating?

A method of duplicating which uses the principle that oil and water do not mix. A master is made with a greasy impression which will pick up a greasy ink but the rest of the plate is dampened with water and rejects the ink.

The impression is off-set onto a rotating blanket – where of course it comes out in reverse. Later on its circuit the impression on the blanket is offset again onto the copy paper which gives a reverse image of the reverse image. The final copy is therefore printed the right way round, and can be read.

2 How many copies can be obtained from an offset master?

A paper plate may give up to about 5 000 copies; a plastic plate up to about 10 000; while a metal plate can give up to 50 000.

3 What are the advantages of offset duplicating?

(a) There is a high quality of reproduction. (b) Large runs of copies can be reproduced. (c) The cost reduces over long runs to little more than the cost of the paper used.

4 What are the disadvantages of offset duplicating?

(a) The machine is relatively expensive to buy. (b) More training in operating the machine is necessary than for other methods. (c) It is uneconomical for short runs.

5 How does stencil duplicating work?

The master copy for this form of duplicating is a stencil. Ink is forced through impressions cut into the stencil, which are reproduced on copy paper beneath. For this reason, stencil duplicating is known also as ink duplicating.

6 How are stencils prepared?

In several ways: (a) By hand, using a stylus; (b) With a typewriter; (c) By using an electronic stencil scanner; (d) With a thermal heat copier.

7 What are the parts of a stencil?

(a) The head, which contains perforations used for fixing the stencil to the duplicator. (b) The stencil sheet which is covered with a wax or plastic coating through which ink will not pass. (c) The backing sheet which gives a flat surface so that impressions are good on the stencil sheet. (d) A carbon paper which presses against the back of the stencil sheet to give a dark background to aid checking.

8 How can mistakes be corrected when typing a stencil?

By painting over the error with correcting fluid. When the fluid has dried, the word can be retyped.

9 How is a stencil prepared on a typewriter?

(a) The ribbon is disengaged, so that the type faces strike directly onto the stencil. (b) The stencil sheet is perforated by the action of the type faces. (c) When typing is complete, the stencil must be carefully checked. It is easier to correct one stencil than 500 copies.

10 How is a stencil cut by using a thermal heat copier?

The copier works by heat absorbed by the black lettering which eats into the stencil. It only works with carbon based types. The original document and the stencil are both passed through the copier, to give an exact copy.

11 How is a stencil cut with an electronic scanner?

The stencil is placed in the scanner alongside the original document to be copied and the machine uses a photoelectric cell and cutting stylus to prepare the stencil. The machine is fully automatic and a perfect stencil is reproduced in a few minutes.

12 Describe how copies are reproduced on a stencil duplicator

(a) The stencil is fastened over the drum of the machine. The ink is inside the drum. (b) The ink is fed through the perforations in the stencil and onto the absorbent paper below.

13 What are the advantages of stencil duplicating?

(a) A large number of copies can be obtained from each stencil. (b) The quality of the copies is good. (c) A stencil duplicator is easy to operate. (d) Alterations to the stencil can easily be made.

Written Exercise: *Write a short account of stencil duplicating from the secretary's point of view. In your answer refer particularly to: (a) Positioning the work on the stencil; (b) The signature box on a letter — how would this have to be done? (c) How to check and correct a stencil.*

Go over the topic again until you are sure of all the answers. Then tick it off on the check list at the back of the book.

15 Meetings – 1: personnel

1 Why are meetings held?

To assist communication and decision making in a particular field or area of organisation.

2 List the chief types of meetings to be held in a large company

(a) Statutory meetings. (b) Annual General Meetings. (c) Extraordinary General Meetings. (d) Board meetings. (e) Committee meetings. (f) Departmental meetings.

3 Distinguish between a formal meeting and an informal meeting

A formal meeting is one called in accordance with a given set of rules – perhaps as laid down by Parliament or by a governing body of some sort. Minutes will be taken and a set procedure will be followed.

Informal meetings are freed of such restrictions, people may speak their minds without fear of being quoted on the matter and the intention is to clear the air and reduce tension by an open, unrestricted discussion.

4 What is a statutory meeting?

One required by Act of Parliament, like the first meeting of a limited company under the Companies Act 1985.

5 What is an AGM?

An Annual General Meeting, laid down in the rules of most companies, clubs, etc. as a formal meeting to review the year's activities, consider the finances of the organisation, give an opportunity for the Board of a company or the Committee of the club to be revised in membership, etc.

6 Who is in charge of a meeting?

The Chairman, who may be of either sex.

7 List the Chairman's functions

(a) To authorise the calling of a meeting. (b) To preside over it when it assembles and call it to order at the start. (c) To conduct it in a proper manner with remarks being made impersonally through the Chair and not in a personal way from one member to another directly. (d) To put motions, amendments, etc. in a proper manner. (e) To close the meeting in an appropriate way after fixing the date of the next meeting if agreeable. (f) To liaise with the Secretary, or the Minuting Secretary if a separate person, to ensure that the minutes are correct before they are reproduced for circulation and approval at the next meeting.

8 What are the Treasurer's functions?

To handle the finances of the club or organisation; to collect subscriptions; to approve expenditure; to pay bills and keep accounts; to prepare a Receipts and Payments Account for presentation at the AGM; to explain this statement to the members and report on the financial position.

9 What are the functions of committee members?

To participate in the work of the Committee; to represent those whose interests they are appointed to serve by making representations, proposing motions or amendments to motions; avoid personal conflicts by observing the rules of behaviour, speaking through the Chair, etc.

10 What is a Standing Committee?

A permanent committee, like a Safety Committee or an Industrial Relations Committee, which meets regularly. Such a committee handles such problems as arise in its field from time to time, and keeps the whole area of activity open for discussion at any time.

11 What is an *ad hoc* committee?

The phrase means 'for this particular purpose'. It is a short-lived committee formed to deal with a particular problem – perhaps an accident or a disciplinary matter or a particular event such as a royal or presidential visit.

Written Exercise: *The Chairman of a public meeting discussing an environmental issue is concerned by the unruly nature of the meeting. He interrupts a speaker to say: 'I insist, ladies and gentlemen, that this discussion be made through the Chair, and not in an unruly way'. What does he/she mean? Explain fully.*

Go over the topic again until you are sure of all the answers. Then tick it off on the check list at the back of the book.

16 Meetings – 2: documents and duties

1 What is a 'notice' in the context of meetings?

Either a personal letter sent to a member of a committee, or a poster – like a public announcement for display on a notice-board announcing the calling of a meeting.

2 You have to circulate a notice to members of a committee. What details should be included?

(a) The date, time and venue (the place where the meeting will be held). (b) The purpose of the meeting – unless an agenda is enclosed, or is mentioned as 'agenda to follow'. (c) The minutes of the previous meeting unless already circulated. (d) The circulation of the notice – so that members know who else is expected to attend.

3 What is an agenda?

A detailed list of items to be discussed. It forms the basis for the conduct of the meeting; the Chairman dealing with the items in the sequence given in the agenda and moving on to the next item if the discussion on a particular item is concluded.

4 Certain items come at the very beginning of an agenda. What are they?

(a) Apologies for absence   If you are going to be absent you should send the Chairman a memo explaining why. Last minute apologies may be conveyed at the meeting on your behalf by a member who *is* present.
(b) Minutes of the previous meeting   These should be read out – which can be a tedious business – but if they have been circulated previously anyone may propose 'that the minutes be taken as read'.
(c) Matters arising   These are matters arising from the minutes – members may

want to know what happened about some decision taken at the last meeting, etc. The Chairman may halt such discussion at once if the matter arising appears on the agenda lower down, because a full discussion of developments will take place at that point in the meeting.

5 What are the final items on most agendas?

(a) Any other business Usually written AOB. This gives an opportunity for any member to raise any point he/she likes. It is generally used for brief items which can be quickly dealt with – for example to acquaint the committee with news of the death of a former member. The Chairman will send a letter of condolence or a floral tribute, or arrange for attendance at the funeral by a representative.

(b) Date of next meeting This is a good opportunity to fill in a date in everyone's diary before it gets too congested.

6 How is an agenda prepared?

(a) The secretary will prepare the agenda after liaison with the Chairman who will have a strong influence over the items to be discussed at a particular meeting. (b) The introductory items – apologies etc. always appear. (c) The Chairman will usually have 2 or 3 items for the agenda based on follow-up procedures from earlier meetings. He/she will also usually know of new items that have arisen in the meantime. (d) Other members who wish to have an item discussed should draw it to the attention of the Secretary – usually a deadline would be set of, say, 2 weeks before the meeting. The Secretary will then draw it to the Chairman's attention. If not accepted as an agenda item it may still be raised under AOB – any other business. (e) The Secretary will

then draw up a draft agenda which the Chairman may revise – perhaps by changing the order of items, etc.
(f) Finally, the amended agenda will be duplicated and circulated.

7 What is a Chairman's agenda?

It is a special agenda made out for the Chairman's use which contains more information than the ordinary agenda.

8 What sort of extra information?

It might refer to the numbers of earlier reports on the matter, or official publications, statutory instruments, etc. Copies of relevant rules, previous documents by the Committee, etc. might be noted. On the right-hand side, space would be provided for notes to be made by the Chairman which would be useful in follow-up activities, and in the preparation and checking of the minutes.

9 What are minutes?

They are a brief record of the proceedings of a meeting, designed to keep a clear, accurate record of business transacted.

10 Who takes the minutes?

Usually the Secretary, but where the Secretary has important organisational activities and no secretarial skills (as with many clubs and societies) a minuting secretary who does have the skills should be appointed.

11 What are the chief points to remember when taking minutes?

(a) A verbatim report of everything that is said is *not* required. (b) The minutes will start with a brief description of the meeting, the names of those present with the Chairman first and the officers last – ordinary members in between. A list of apologies for absence. (c) A note that the minutes were read, or taken as read, and were signed by the Chairman as a true record. (d) Matters arising should be noted. (e) Correspondence may include noteworthy items. (f) Then come the agenda items in turn, with a careful note of any resolutions, amendments, and decisions. If any duty is imposed upon, or voluntarily assumed by, any member, a note should be made and the matter can then be followed up. (g) Any other business.

12 What type of language should be used when drawing up the minutes?

Temperate language, which will not 'colour' the minutes. For example to record 'a violent discussion arose' would not be appropriate. 'A lively debate followed' would be a better choice of words.

13 What is the custom with regard to capital letters in minutes?

It is usual to capitalise all names and official positions, such as Chairman, Secretary, Treasurer, etc.

14 What are the Secretary's duties after the meeting?

(a) To collect any papers, pencils, etc. left behind and clear the room for use by the next group meeting there. (b) To go through any notes made at the meeting and take action on them (e.g. it may have been decided to ask someone not present to do something on the Committee's behalf. (c) The Chairman may wish memos of thanks to be sent to those outsiders who attended to give reports, or advise on certain matters. (d) Draft minutes should be prepared and submitted to the Chairman for his/her comments. (e) If agreed, copies should then be printed and circulated, or if delayed a memo should be made to trigger off the duplication at a future date. (f) The date of the next meeting should be inserted into all relevant diaries and year planners. (g) If refreshments were served, a memo thanking the Catering Department should be sent and any chit

for costing purposes should be passed
to the Chairman for authorisation.

Written Exercise: *Draft an agenda and a notice for a Safety Committee meeting. The three chief items for discussion are 'car parking', 'fume disposal at the warehouse' (where fork-lift trucks are in use) and 'overhead cables'. A special item is the death of a workman P. T. Smith who was crushed by a reversing lorry in the loading bay. Include in the circulation list 8 people as departmental representatives, and state their departments. Invent names for the Chairman, Secretary and Minuting Secretary.*

Go over the topic again until you are sure of all the answers. Then tick it off on the check list at the back of the book.

17 Meetings – 3: terminology

1 What does the word 'terminology' mean?

It means 'specialised vocabulary' – the special words used in any particular activity – in this case when organising a meeting.

2 What slang word do we use to describe specialist terminology?

It is called jargon.

3 Should we sneer at jargon?

No – we should learn the specialised vocabulary.

4 What is a quorum?

The minimum number of members that must be present at a meeting under the rules, if the proceedings are to be valid.

5 What does 'ex officio' mean?

'By virtue of office'. An official may automatically qualify for a position because of the office he/she holds. Thus the mayor of a borough is ex officio a Justice of the Peace during his/her tenure of office. Similarly a personnel officer may be ex officio a member of the Industrial Relations Committee of a company.

6 What does the word 'co-opt' mean?

Co-option is the power of a committee to ask others to serve on the committee if it seems that their expertise will be helpful. Usually a person may be co-opted by a simple majority vote of the committee.

7 What is a 'motion'?

A motion is a proposition for consideration at a meeting. It should normally be written out and handed to the Chairman or Secretary in advance, so that it can be included in the agenda – but as a matter of urgency a motion may be introduced at a meeting, if the meeting agrees.

8 Who speaks to the motion?

The **proposer**, who is followed by the **seconder**. A discussion then follows and the proposer has the right to reply to the discussion.

9 What is an amendment?

It is a suggestion to alter the wording of a motion during the course of discussion to make it more acceptable to the meeting, or cover some point omitted in the original motion. It must be proposed and seconded. If there is no seconder it is not proceeded with. If the amendment is carried the motion is forthwith amended.

10 What is a resolution?

It is a formal decision carried at a meeting. It is proposed, seconded and carried – i.e. passed by a majority vote.

11 What ways may a resolution be carried?

(a) Unanimously – everyone in agreement. (b) *Nem. con.* – no one contradicting. Some people voted in favour, and no one against, but some people did not vote. (c) By a majority – say 8:3 or 7:5. The majority required may be specified in the rules. (d) By the Chairman's casting vote – if voting is exactly equal, the Chairman is allowed a second vote to resolve the difficulty.

12 What does the phrase 'through the Chair' mean?

At a meeting all remarks are made to the Chair. You begin your contribution with the words 'Mr Chairman' or 'Madam Chairman'. You may not speak across the table directly to another person, or engage in side discussions while someone else is speaking to the Chair.

13 What does the phrase 'lie on the table' mean?

It is used when no further action will be taken on a letter, document or motion at this particular meeting. The matter will then be given time for developments to take place, and may be raised at the next meeting if anyone is interested.

14 What does a proposal that 'the meeting proceeds to the next business' mean?

It means that the matter under discussion shall be left for the present — having been well and truly aired and no agreement seeming likely — and that the next item on the agenda should be discussed.

15 What does the phrase 'proposed that the motion be now put' mean?

It means that the discussion in the view of the proposer has gone on long enough and that the Chairman should put it to the vote. If this is carried, the proposer of the original motion is allowed to reply to the discussion and then the motion is voted upon.

16 What are 'standing orders'?

A body of rules, built up over the years or agreed to from the start of an organisation (in a constitution) which governs the procedure of the organisation's affairs, and particularly the conduct of meetings.

17 What does 'on a point of order, Mr Chairman!' mean?

It is a way of interrupting procedures if the rules of conduct are not being observed. Thus if a member is abusive, or calls another member a liar, or makes personal remarks about someone who is not present, or if the Chairman does not follow procedure, any member may stop proceedings to draw the attention of the meeting to the breach of the rules. A common case is absence of a quorum – as where some members leave early.

18 What is an 'adjournment'?

It is the breaking-off of a meeting, to postpone further discussion or because of shortage of time. The Chairman proposes an adjournment and if the meeting agrees, discussion will proceed at a later meeting, for which adequate notice will be given.

Written Exercise: *Draw up a short constitution for a drama society, tennis club or other recreational body, mentioning the rights and duties of members, the membership of the committee and the frequency and conduct of meetings.*

Go over the topic again until you are sure of all the answers. Then tick it off on the check list at the back of the book.

18 Receipts and payments – 1: bank current accounts

1 What is a current account?

An account into which money can be put – by means of a paying-in slip – or withdrawn – by the use of cheques and other methods of payment. The word 'current' comes from the French *courrant* (running) – and denotes an account with a running balance.

2 Here is a current account. Explain the running balance

D. G. Brown, 21 Hall Street, Newtown.

Debit £	Credit £	Balance £
–	–	174.50
24.50		150.00
32.50		117.50
	240.84	358.34
500.00		141.66Dr

(a) When the balance shows a figure by itself – as with £174.50 opposite – it is a credit balance. This means that the customer of the bank is owed money by the bank because he/she has deposited money with it. (b) A debit entry means that the customer has received value – usually by drawing a cheque. This reduces the balance on the account. (c) A credit entry means that the customer has given more funds to the bank, by making out a paying-in slip or in some other way. This increases the balance on the account. (d) If the withdrawals are greater than the sum available the balance becomes a debit balance, and the letters Dr appear – meaning the customer is a debtor – the account is overdrawn.

3 How can money be credited to an account?

(a) By the customer or his agent paying money in by means of a paying-in slip. (b) By credit transfer under the bank giro system – this transfers money from another branch or another bank. For example many firms pay their wages this way.

4 What is the document shown in Fig. 18.1?

It is a paying-in slip.

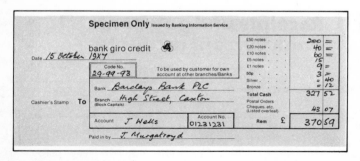

Fig. 18.1 A paying-in slip

5 How may money be withdrawn from an account, giving a debit entry on the account?

(a) By the customer or his/her known representative presenting a cheque over the counter. (b) By making a cheque out to a third party who presents it (if it is an open cheque) or clears it through the banking mechanism (if it is a crossed cheque). (c) By a direct debit arrangement. (d) By a standing order arrangement. (e) By electronic means through a cash dispenser or home service terminal.

6 What is a direct debit arrangement?

It is an arrangement used when the amount of a regular payment varies from time to time – as with rates to local authorities. The customer signs a direct-debit mandate giving the third party the right to ask for its money direct, since it knows how much to ask for. The bank then deducts it from the account and the customer finds out later.

7 What is a standing order arrangement?

This is used where the sum payable is the same every month, as with loan repayments, mortgages, etc. The bank is given a standing instruction to pay the sum due every month.

8 Your office has received 20 cheques from customers today. What is the procedure?

(a) The cheques would go up to the cashier after being received by the mail inwards department. (b) The cashier would enter them in the Cash Book, in the Bank Account, and then prepare the paying-in slip. (c) When entered in the paying-in book (which is a collection of paying-in slips) the cheques will be taken to the bank and paid in. The cashier at the bank will stamp the duplicate in the book and initial it after checking the addition.

9 Two of the cheques are open and one is a bearer cheque. How would you safeguard them?

The open cheques should be crossed. The bearer cheque should be endorsed 'Pay to the account of . . .'

10 What sort of cheque is shown in Fig. 18.2? What is its significance?

It is a crossed cheque. Such a cheque cannot be cashed over the counter (except by the customer personally) but must be cleared into a bank account.

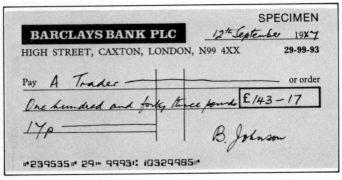

Fig. 18.2 A crossed cheque

11 What is an 'account payee' cheque?

It is a cheque which has the words 'a/c payee' written in the crossing. This is a general crossing, but it suggests that the bank only clears the cheque into the account of the named payee.

12 Why only 'suggests'?

Because it can be cleared into another account but the bank is 'put upon enquiry' into the matter. This means that it must check that the payee has given authority for the cheque to be paid in elsewhere.

13 What is a special crossing?

A cheque which names the bank which the cheque is to be cleared into, for example Newtown University a/c, Lloyds Bank, Newtown.

Written Exercise: *Make out a paying-in slip similar to the one in Fig. 18.1 with 5 cheques entered.*

Go over the topic again until you are sure of all the answers. Then tick it off on the check list at the back of the book.

19 Receipts and payments – 2: the petty cash book

1 What is the petty cash book?

A specially ruled book which enables a young person to take care of small items of cash, using a system called the imprest system.

2 How does the imprest system work?

The chief cashier decides how much cash is required for one week to run the simple day-to-day expenses of the office (e.g. postage, messenger's fares and minor payments of all sorts). Suppose this is £50 per week. It becomes the 'imprest', the sum of money given to the petty cashier, and recorded in the petty cash book. At the end of the week, once all payments have been recorded, the cashier checks the book and restores the imprest to its original £50 ready for the next week.

3 How is the petty cash book ruled?

As shown in Fig. 19.1.

4 Explain the ruling

(a) The 'centre' of the page is offset towards the left-hand side. (b) The debit side is reduced to a single money column, and the details about the debit entries are written in the details column on the credit side. (c) The credit side is extended to include several analysis columns. Only the first column headed 'Total' is the real credit side of the account, in which all money paid out (credit the giver) is entered. Each amount is then analysed off into columns where the various expenses can be collected together, postage, travelling expenses, etc. The last column, 'Ledger A/Cs', is different from the rest,

Debit Side   Credit Side PCB 17

£	p	Date	Details	PCV	Total £	p	Postage £	p	Travelling £	p	Stationery £	p	Sundry Expenses £	p	Ledger A/Cs £	p
100	00	19.. Apr. 4	Imprest received	CB174												
		4	Postage stamps	1	27	30	27	30								
		5	Train fares (Reading)	2	9	65			9	65						
		5	Envelopes	3	13	65					13	65				
		6	Recorded delivery letters	4	4	25	4	25								
		6	Cleaning materials	5	3	65							3	65		
		6	Bus fares	6	11	68			11	68						
		7	Refreshments for visitors	7	8	26							8	26		
		7	T. Smith	8	11	24									11	24
18	12	8	Telephone cash received	£42												
		8	Gratuity (rubbish clearance)	9	1	11							1	11		
		9	Postage stamps	10	14	25	14	25								
					93	93	45	80	10	33	13	65	12	91	11	24
		9	Balance	c/d	24	49	(£25)		(£33)		(£13)		(£73)		(£17)	
£118	42				£118	42										
24	49	11	Balance	b/d												
75	51	11	Imprest restored by cashier	CB187												

Fig. 19.1 The ruling of a petty cash book

56

and has a separate column for folio numbers alongside it.

5 What did the petty cashier do on 4 April?

Drew the imprest of £100 and paid postage £27.30.

6 What happened on 8 April?

The petty cashier collected cash from members of staff for private telephone calls – and also gave the dustman a tip for clearing rubbish.

7 On balancing the book on 9 April what should we find about the various totals in the analysis columns?

They should cross-tot to come to the same result as the Total column.

8 What happens to the total of the Postage column?

It is debited in the postage account as one of the losses (expenses) of the business.

9 What happens to the £11.24 paid to T Smith

It is debited in T Smith's account. He was a creditor, but we have now paid him the money in cash to clear the account. Debit Smith, as he has received money.

10 What happens to the £18.42 telephone money collected?

The money itself is in the petty cashier's till and will offset some of the expenditure. The £18.42 is posted to the credit side of the telephone account (L42). It reduces the expenditure for telephones when we come to do the final accounts at the end of the year.

11 Why does the cashier only need to restore the £75.51 at the end of the week, when the petty cashier spent £93.93?

Because the difference (£18.42) was collected from the staff for telephone calls.

12 What are the advantages of the imprest system?

(a) It saves the chief cashier being bothered for trifling sums of money.
(b) It is good training for a young person, with a simple method of bookkeeping.
(c) The small sum involved is not much of a temptation to either another

member of staff or to the petty cashier.
(d) The analysis columns collect many
small items together and reduce posting
to the ledger – they can all be done in
one entry.

Written Exercise: *Rule up a petty cash book the same as Fig. 19.1 and make the following entries. Balance the account at the end of the week.*

Mar 1 Balance b/d £45.50 and imprest
of £54.50 restored (to bring to
£100).

Mar 2 Stationery expenses £4.25; paid
for coffee, tea, etc., £2.10.

Mar 3 Paid for stamps £11.60; staff
fares £8.60.

Mar 4 Paid traveller's hotel expenses
£15.50; collected £4.75 from a
staff member for an international
call (telephone a/c).

Mar 5 Paid for stationery £12.30;
postage £4.50.

Go over the topic again until you are sure of all the answers. Then tick it off on the check list at the back of the book.

20 Security in the office

**1 What are the security
problems in offices?**

(a) The security of cash and valuables.
(b) The security of ideas, inventions,
discoveries, financial position, etc.
(c) Confidentiality in personal and
business affairs. (d) The possibilities of
terrorism.

**2 What is the correct attitude to
all such problems?**

Eternal vigilance. Without getting
paranoid about security we must always
be on the alert for theft, embezzlement,
burglary, industrial and commercial

espionage, computer theft, and terrorism.

3 What is theft?

Dishonestly appropriating the property of another with the intention of permanently depriving the other of it (Theft Act 1968 S.1).

4 How can we prevent theft?

(a) By using security methods of bookkeeping where possible, such as the imprest system of Petty Cash described in Topic 19. (b) By devising safe systems of paying in cash takings — tills emptied regularly of large notes — security movements to banks at irregular intervals by different routes. (c) By adequate manning of reception areas; booking visitors in and out; escorting visitors around the building and passing them out through reception and car parking areas.

5 What is industrial espionage?

It is the theft of industrial and commercial expertise by skilled observers, often with photographic memories or concealed cameras, tape recorders, etc.

6 What sort of people should we suspect?

Almost everyone, from the opportunist sneak-thief who sees an opportunity — an office door left open, an office window giving access — and pops in to see whether there is anything worth seeing or worth knowing, to the sophisticated and organised spy who comes prepared and knows exactly what he/she is after. Visitors of every type, customers, competitors, people seeking appointments with no genuine motive or past record of links with the firm should be suspected. Potential employees who failed to take up appointments offered may not have been genuine applicants. Make a record of visitors and preserve it – so that even months later you can check back who might have been the spy.

7 What is burglary?

Entering a building or other occupied place to commit theft or cause grievous bodily harm, or actually doing so after entering as a trespasser.

8 How can we prevent burglary, or reduce the effects?

(a) By proper attention to locking up premises, the safe custody of keys, security checks on the backgrounds of those supplied with keys whether on the staff or outsiders (decorators, builders, plumbers, etc.). (b) By a security burglar alarm system. (c) By liaison with the local crime prevention officer about all security aspects affecting the firm. (d) By a standing committee reporting back to Board level on all security aspects – probably through the general administration officer or some similar senior member of staff.

9 From the secretary's viewpoint what aspects of security are important?

(a) The whole question of confidentiality – much correspondence is confidential, and so are the minutes of meetings. (b) The personal affairs of one's chief are confidential unless a higher loyalty – to the firm or company – raises a conflict of loyalties. This is a very difficult area.

Written Exercise: *It is proposed to manufacture a specialist computer unit which will have an ordinary household use but may also have uses in military defence programmes. Consider the security problems likely to arise with: (a) design staff; (b) technician staff; (c) safeguarding working drawings; (d) industrial and military espionage. List the measures you would take to safeguard each area.*

Go over the topic again until you are sure of all the answers. Then tick it off on the check list at the back of the book.